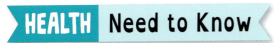

HEALTH Need to Know

Social Health and Friendships

by Ashley Kuehl

Consultant: Caitlin Krieck, Social Studies Teacher and Instructional Coach, The Lab School of Washington

BEARPORT
PUBLISHING

Minneapolis, Minnesota

Credits

Cover and title page, © CarlosBarquero/Adobe Stock; 3, © irin-k/Shutterstock; 5, © IPGGutenbergUKLtd/iStock; 7, © igor_kell/iStock; 8, © Dean Drobot/Shutterstock; 9, © monkeybusinessimages/iStock; 11, © aldomurillo/iStock; 13, © MTStock Studio/iStock; 15, © AS photo family/Shutterstock; 17, © Prostock-studio/Shutterstock; 19, © Lock Stock/Getty Images; 21, © Ground Picture/Shutterstock; 23, © skynesher/iStock; 25, © New Africa/Shutterstock; 27, © aldomurillo/iStock; 28, © Forgem/Shutterstock.

Bearport Publishing Company Product Development Team

Publisher: Jen Jenson; Director of Product Development: Spencer Brinker; Editorial Director: Allison Juda; Editor: Cole Nelson; Editor: Tiana Tran; Production Editor: Naomi Reich; Art Director: Kim Jones; Designer: Kayla Eggert; Designer: Steve Scheluchin; Production Specialist: Owen Hamlin

Statement on Usage of Generative Artificial Intelligence

Bearport Publishing remains committed to publishing high-quality nonfiction books. Therefore, we restrict the use of generative AI to ensure accuracy of all text and visual components pertaining to a book's subject. See BearportPublishing.com for details.

Library of Congress Cataloging-in-Publication Data is available at www.loc.gov or upon request from the publisher.

ISBN: 979-8-89577-077-1 (hardcover)
ISBN: 979-8-89577-524-0 (paperback)
ISBN: 979-8-89577-194-5 (ebook)

Copyright © 2026 Bearport Publishing Company. All rights reserved. No part of this publication may be reproduced in whole or in part, stored in any retrieval system, or transmitted in any form or by any means, electronic, mechanical, photocopying, recording, or otherwise, without written permission from the publisher. Bearport Publishing is a division of FlutterBee Education Group.

For more information, write to Bearport Publishing, 3500 American Blvd W, Suite 150, Bloomington, MN 55431.

Contents

Hanging Out. 4

Part of a Whole 6

People All Around 10

Clear Words, Clear Actions 12

I'll Be There. 16

Why We Need People. 18

Make It Better 22

People Need People. 26

Tips for Building Social Health 28

SilverTips for Success 29

Glossary 30

Read More 31

Learn More Online 31

Index .32

About the Author 32

Hanging Out

What do you do when you hang out with friends? Do you go to the mall? Or maybe you play video games together. These are great ways to have fun. But did you know they are good for you, too? Time with friends is part of your **social** health.

Social health is more than just **interacting** with people you know. It has to do with everybody around you. This involves people you don't know.

Part of a Whole

Health is made up of many parts. One part is physical health. This includes eating well, exercising, and getting enough sleep. Mental health is also important. It's the way a person feels in their mind. Social health is another part.

People need a balance in all areas of health. Too much of one part can mean too little of another. This can make a person sick.

What is social health? It's wellness that comes from connections with people. Good social health involves being part of strong **communities**. This may include people who live or work together. It can also involve bonds with friends and family.

Sometimes, people need a break from others. Social health can also include spending time alone. This gives people space to gather their thoughts and feelings.

Many neighborhoods have a strong sense of community.

People All Around

A person's social health is shaped by those around them. Different people help us learn, grow, and practice social health throughout our lives. Often, our family members are the first people to teach us how to treat others. As we get older, we get new connections. Teachers and friends help us learn more.

Every connection you have with others is special in its own way. You may act differently with your parents than with your friends or classmates. Over time, you learn the differences.

Clear Words, Clear Actions

One important part of healthy bonds is **communication**. This allows people to **express** themselves. They can feel free to show who they really are. And they can ask for what they need.

Communication also means listening and understanding. It includes paying attention to others' feelings, words, and actions.

Good communication includes **consent**. People need to agree to what does or does not happen. Both sides respect each others' decisions.

Communication doesn't mean people always agree. It's normal to have different opinions. However, good communication skills can help people work through problems together. Sometimes, people need to **negotiate**. They give and take until they can agree to something they are both okay with.

When people negotiate, neither side gets everything they want. They might have to give up some things so both sides can be happy.

I'll Be There

One way to strengthen connections with others is to be there for them. Spend time with people you care about. Pay attention to what's happening in their lives. Show up for big events. Relationships are a two-way street. Both sides must make an effort.

Social media connects people who live far apart. This can be good. But ignoring people in real life to spend time online can harm your social health. Find a balance between the two.

Why We Need People

Being part of healthy communities gives people a sense of **belonging**. This makes them feel valued, loved, and needed. Having no connections may make people feel lonely. In a 2022 survey, about half of U.S. adults said they felt lonely. Sadly, the numbers were even higher for younger adults.

When a person feels like they belong, their brain releases chemicals that make them feel good. It gives them energy to take care of themselves.

During hard times, people need support. Having strong connections with others can make facing challenges easier.

Turning to friends, family, and other community members can help **emotionally**. These supporters may offer advice. They can help find a solution to a problem. Sometimes, having someone listen to your worries is all you need.

Emotional health is often tied to social health. Having strong bonds tends to make it easier to share emotions.

Make It Better

There are many ways to improve social health. Creating new connections is a great one. Do something different to meet new people. Try a hobby or sport. Having common interests helps people form bonds with one another.

Doing something new can be hard. But working through challenges helps people feel better about themselves. It helps their brains work better, too.

Seek out ways to help others within communities you are a part of. Volunteering at an animal shelter is one way. Another is raking the leaves in a neighbor's yard. Helping others can help you form new bonds. It also makes you feel good.

How can you start volunteering? Search online for local needs. Check out schools, churches, or senior centers. Ask a grown-up if you want help reaching out.

Many animal shelters rely on volunteers.

People Need People

Making connections with others is important. The people around you **influence** your social health. Good social health can help people form strong bonds.

It's your responsibility to take care of your health. But you don't have to do it alone!

Everybody is different. How you care for your social health may be unique to you. Figure out which connections will make you the best you can be.

Tips for Building Social Health

1. Be honest and kind when talking with others.

2. If you need something, ask for it.

3. Practice saying no when something feels unsafe or wrong.

4. Offer to do a task for someone else.

5. Try something new. Join an activity or club.

6. Find a balance between communicating online and in real life.

7. Join a neighborhood clean-up.

8. Build connections across multiple communities.

9. Volunteer at a community center, church, or hospital.

10. Find common interests with others.

SilverTips for SUCCESS

★ SilverTips for REVIEW

Review what you've learned. Use the text to help you.

Define key terms

communication
community
connection
negotiate
social health

Check for understanding

Why is communication important?

How can people improve their social health?

What benefits can come from good social health?

Think deeper

How would you describe your own social health? What steps might you take to improve it?

★ SilverTips on TEST-TAKING

- **Make a study plan.** Ask your teacher what the test is going to cover. Then, set aside time to study a little bit every day.

- **Read all the questions carefully.** Be sure you know what is being asked.

- **Skip any questions** you don't know how to answer right away. Mark them and come back later if you have time.

Glossary

belonging fitting in or feeling like part of a group

communication the act of sharing information, ideas, or feelings with others

communities groups of people who share places, beliefs, or interests in common

consent to say yes to something

emotionally in a way that has to do with feelings

express to show what one feels or thinks

influence to have an effect on someone or something

interacting being with or talking with others

negotiate to work on reaching an agreement

social having to do with people being together

Read More

Finne, Stephanie. *Communities (Building Relationships).* Minneapolis: Jump!, 2025.

Holmes, Kirsty. *Healthy Mind (Live Well!).* Minneapolis: Bearport Publishing, 2024.

Ratzer, Mary. *Connecting with Others (Spotlight on a Fair and Equal Society).* Buffalo, NY: Rosen Publishing, 2022.

Learn More Online

1. Go to **FactSurfer.com** or scan the QR code below.

2. Enter "**Social Health and Friendships**" into the search box.

3. Click on the cover of this book to see a list of websites.

Index

belonging 18

communication 12–14, 28

community 8–9, 18, 20, 24, 28

connections 8, 10, 16, 18, 20, 22, 26, 28

consent 13

family 8, 10, 20

feelings 6, 8, 12, 18, 22, 24

friends 4, 8, 10, 20

listening 12, 20

mental health 6

negotiate 14

physical health 6

school 24

volunteering 24, 28

About the Author

Ashley Kuehl is an editor and writer specializing in nonfiction for young people. She lives in Minneapolis, MN.